# Winter Fun

Katie Peters

GRL Consultants,
Diane Craig and Monica Marx,
Certified Literacy Specialists

Lerner Publications ◆ Minneapolis

**Note from a GRL Consultant**
This Pull Ahead leveled book has been carefully designed for beginning readers. A team of guided reading literacy experts has reviewed and leveled the book to ensure readers pull ahead and experience success.

Lerner Publications Company
A division of Lerner Publishing Group, Inc.
241 First Avenue North
Minneapolis, MN 55401 USA

For reading levels and more information, look up this title at www.lernerbooks.com.

Main body text set in Memphis Pro 24/39
Typeface provided by Linotype.

Photo Acknowledgments
The images in this book are used with the permission of: © Shutterstock, pp. 3, 6–7, 8–9, 16 (top right), 16 (bottom right); © iStockphoto, pp. 4–5, 10–11, 12–13, 14–15, 16 (top left), 16 (top center), 16 (bottom left)

Front cover: © iStockphoto

**Library of Congress Cataloging-in-Publication Data**

Names: Peters, Katie, author.
Title: Winter fun / Katie Peters.
Description: Minneapolis, MN : Lerner Publications, [2020] | Series: Seasons all around me (Pull ahead readers - Nonfiction) | Includes index.
Identifiers: LCCN 2018058178 (print) | LCCN 2018060467 (ebook) | ISBN 9781541562387 (eb pdf) | ISBN 9781541558694 (lb : alk. paper) | ISBN 9781541573475 (pb : alk. paper)
Subjects: LCSH: Winter—Juvenile literature. | Snow—Juvenile literature. | Seasons—Juvenile literature.
Classification: LCC QB637.8 (ebook) | LCC QB637.8 .P4785 2020 (print) | DDC 508.2—dc23

LC record available at https://lccn.loc.gov/2018058178

Manufactured in the United States of America
1 – CG – 7/15/19

# Contents

# Winter Fun

You can make a snow hill.

You can make a snowball.

You can make a
snow person.

You can make a snow fort.

You can make a
snow angel.

You can have fun
in the winter.

# Did You See It?

snow angel

snowball

snow fort

snow hill

snow person

# Index